FIERCE

Women of the Bible Who Changed the World

A BIBLE STUDY BY

JENNIFER COWART

JENNY YOUNGMAN, CONTRIBUTOR

Abingdon Women/Nashville

Fierce
Women of the Bible Who Changed the World
Leader Guide

ISBN 978-1-5018-8292-0

19 20 21 22 23 24 25 26 27 28—10 9 8 7 6 5 4 3 2 1
MANUFACTURED IN THE UNITED STATES OF AMERICA

Contents

About the Author

Jennifer Cowart is the executive pastor at Harvest Church, a United Methodist congregation in Warner Robins, Georgia, that she and her husband, Jim, began in 2001. With degrees in Christian education, counseling, and business, she has been integral to the development of the Emerging and Discipleship Ministries at Harvest, including more than three hundred small groups that meet in homes and workplaces. As a gifted Bible teacher and speaker, Jen brings biblical truth to life through humor, authenticity, and everyday application. She is the author of the Bible study *Messy People: Life Lessons from Imperfect Biblical Heroes* and coauthor with her husband, Jim, of several small group studies, including *Hand Me Downs* and *Living the Five*. They are the proud parents of two children, Alyssa and Joshua, and have a son-in-law, Andrew.

Follow Jen:

Website: jennifercowart.org or jimandjennifercowart.org
             (check here for event dates and booking information)

     Jim-Jennifer Cowart

ⓘ   jimandjennifercowart

Introduction

The word *fierce* is trendy. It's used to describe women who are extreme athletes, high-level executives, and supermodels. It describes women who are at the top of their game and making a difference in the world. In fact, if you look up the word *fierce* in the dictionary, you'll see adjectives such as "strong," "powerful," "aggressive," and even "savage." That definition makes me think of the wild cats of Africa and India— untamed, dangerous, beautiful, and so powerful. When we hear this description of *fierce*, it may not fit our image of what a beautiful woman of God should be. It may sound too intense or even masculine. But under God's control, a fierce woman of God is a beautiful warrior—not savage or violent but powerful and dangerous in the best sense of the word.

During this six-week study, we are going to dig into fierce women of God in the Bible who lived courageously, obediently, and faithfully in order to fulfill God's plan. Their stories show us the power that comes from resting in God's love and forgiveness—and how this power can lead to amazing things as we lean into His plans for each of us. When we think of fierce women in the Bible, we tend to think of well-known women such as Sarah, Rachel, Ruth, Esther, and Mary, the Mother of Jesus. But in these lessons we will be looking at some lesser-known women such as the midwives of Egypt, Shiphrah and Puah, and Lois and Eunice. Why? Because these women were heroines too. They show us that the faithfulness of ordinary women can change the world. In fact, fierce women such as these have been changing the world for thousands of years. Many have received little recognition, but they lived fiercely anyway. And we can too!

About the Participant Workbook

Before the first session, distribute copies of the participant workbook to the members of your group. Be sure to communicate that they are to complete the first week of readings *before* your first group session. For each week there are five devotional lessons that include both Scripture study as well as reflection and prayer. The lessons are designed to lead women through a quiet time with God where they savor His Word and allow Him to speak to them. Encourage the women in your group to find a quiet place—maybe a favorite chair or a spot on the porch, weather permitting—where they can spend their devotional study time.

Each day the lesson follows the same format: Settle, Focus, Reflect, and Pray. On average the lessons can be completed in about twenty to thirty minutes—depending on how much time is spent in prayer. Completing these readings each week will prepare the women for the discussion and activities of the group session.

About This Leader Guide

As you gather each week with the members of your group, you will have the opportunity to watch video content, discuss and respond to what you're learning, and pray together. You will need access to a television and DVD player with working remotes.

Creating a warm and inviting atmosphere will help to make the women feel welcome. Although optional, you might consider providing snacks for your first meeting and inviting group members to rotate in bringing refreshments each week.

This leader guide and the DVD will be your primary tools for leading each group session. In this book you will find outlines for six group sessions, each formatted for either a 60-minute or 90-minute session:

60-Minute Format

Leader Prep	(Before the session)
Welcome and Opening Prayer	5 minutes
Icebreaker	5 minutes
Video(s)	15–20 minutes
Group Discussion	25 minutes
Closing Prayer	5 minutes

90-Minute Format

Leader Prep	(Before the session)
Welcome and Opening Prayer	5–10 minutes
Icebreaker	5 minutes
Video(s)	15–20 minutes

Group Discussion	30–35 minutes
Deeper Conversation	15 minutes
Closing Prayer	5 minutes

As you can see, the 90-minute format is identical to the 60-minute format but has more time for welcoming/fellowship and group discussion, plus a deeper conversation exercise for small groups. Or your group might prefer to limit the welcoming time and extend the closing prayer time. Feel free to adapt or modify either format, as well as the individual segments and activities, in any way to meet the specific needs and preferences of your group.

Here is a brief overview of the elements included in both formats:

Leader Prep (Before the session)

For your preparation prior to the group session, this section provides an overview of the week's Bible story and theme, the main point of the session, key Scriptures, and a list of materials and equipment needed. Be sure to review this section, as well as the session outline, to plan and prepare before the group meets. If you choose, you also may find it helpful to watch the DVD segment in advance.

Welcome and Opening Prayer (5–10 minutes, depending on session length)

To create a warm, welcoming environment as the women are gathering before the session begins, consider lighting one or more candles, providing coffee or other refreshments, playing worship music, or all of these. (Bring an iPod, smartphone, or tablet and a portable speaker if desired.) Be sure to provide name tags if the women do not know one another or you have new participants in your group. Then, when you are ready to begin, pray the opening prayer that is provided or offer your own.

Icebreaker (5 minutes)

Use the icebreaker to briefly engage the women in the topic while helping them feel comfortable with one another.

Video (15–20 minutes)

Play the "Getting Started: A Devotional Reflection" video (optional), taking a couple of minutes to focus your hearts and minds on God's Word. Then watch the week's teaching video segment together. Be sure to direct participants to the Video Viewer Guide in the participant workbook, which they may complete as they watch the video. (Answers are provided on page 61.)

Group Discussion (25–35 minutes, depending on session length)

After watching the video, choose from the questions provided to facilitate group discussion (questions are provided for both the video and the participant workbook). For the workbook portion, you may choose to read aloud the talking points—*which are excerpts from the participant workbook*—or express them in your own words; then use one or more of the questions that follow to guide your conversation.

Note that more material is provided than you will have time to include. Before the session, select what you want to cover, putting a check mark beside it in your book. Reflect on each question and make some notes in the margins to share during your discussion time. Page references are provided for those questions that relate to specific questions or activities in the participant workbook. For these questions, invite group members to turn in their workbooks to the pages indicated. Participants will need Bibles in order to look up various supplementary Scriptures.

Depending on the number of women in your group and the level of their participation, you may not have time to cover everything you have selected, and that is OK. Rather than attempting to bulldoze through, follow the Spirit's lead and be open to where the Spirit takes the conversation. Remember that your role is not to have all the answers but to encourage discussion and sharing.

Deeper Conversation (15 minutes)

If your group is meeting for 90 minutes, move next to this exercise for deeper sharing in small groups, dividing into groups of two or three. This is a time for women to share more intimately and build connections with one another. (Encourage the women to break into different groups each week.) Before the session, write the question or questions you want to discuss on a marker board or chart paper for all to see. Give a two-minute warning before time is up so that the groups may wrap up their discussion.

Closing Prayer (5 minutes)

Close by leading the group in prayer. Invite the women to briefly name prayer requests. To get things started you might share a personal request of your own. As women share their requests, model for the group by writing each request in your participant workbook, indicating that you will remember to pray for them during the week.

As the study progresses, you might encourage members to participate in the closing prayer by praying out loud for one another and the requests given. Ask the women to volunteer to pray for specific requests, or have each woman pray for the woman on her right or left. Make sure name tags are visible so that group members do not feel awkward if they do not remember someone's name.

After the prayer, remind the women to pray for one another throughout the week.

Before You Begin

As we begin this journey, let's remember that we are meant to be fierce women of God. As we live with the strong sense of knowing who we are in Christ, we will have the courage to live obediently and faithfully into His great, big plans—just like the women we will be studying together. And like them, we can change the world. Let's be fierce!

Jennifer

Basic Leader Helps

Preparing for the Sessions

- Check out your meeting space before each group session. Make sure the room is ready. Do you have enough chairs? Do you have the equipment and supplies you need? (See the list of materials needed in each session outline.)
- Pray for your group and each group member by name. Ask God to work in the life of every woman in your group.
- Read and complete the week's readings in the participant workbook and review the session outline in the leader guide. Put a check mark beside the discussion questions you want to cover and make any notes in the margins that you want to share in your discussion time. If you want, you may also choose to view the video segment.

Leading the Sessions

- Greet each woman personally as she arrives. If desired, take attendance. (This will assist you in identifying members who have missed several sessions so that you may contact them and let them know they were missed.)
- At the start of each session, ask the women to turn off or silence their cell phones.
- Always start on time. Honor the efforts of those who are on time.
- Encourage everyone to participate fully, but don't put anyone on the spot. Invite the women to share as they are comfortable. Be prepared to offer a personal example or answer if no one else responds at first.
- Facilitate but don't dominate. Remember that if you talk most of the time, group members may tend to listen passively rather than engage personally.
- Try not to interrupt, judge, or minimize anyone's comments or input.

- Remember that you are not expected to be the expert or have all the answers. Acknowledge that all of you are on this journey together, with the Holy Spirit as your leader and guide. If issues or questions arise that you don't feel equipped to answer or handle, talk with the pastor or a staff member at your church.
- Encourage good discussion, but don't be timid about calling time on a particular question and moving ahead. Part of your responsibility is to keep the group on track. If you decide to spend extra time on a given question or activity, consider skipping or spending less time on another question or activity in order to stay on schedule.
- Try to end on time. If you are running over, give members the opportunity to leave if they need to. Then wrap up as quickly as you can.
- Be prepared for some women to want to hang out and talk at the end. If you need everyone to leave by a certain time, communicate this at the beginning of the session. If you are meeting in a church during regularly scheduled activities or have arranged for childcare, be sensitive to the agreed-upon ending time.
- Thank the women for coming, and let them know you're looking forward to seeing them next time.

Introductory Session

Note: This session is designed to be 60 minutes in length.

Leader Prep

Overview of the Session

This session is an opportunity to give an overview of the study; get to know one another and share hopes for the study; and handle some housekeeping details such as collecting information for a group roster (name, email address, primary phone number, and, if desired, mailing address), making decisions regarding childcare and refreshments, and distributing books or providing instructions for purchasing. You also will watch a short video and pray together.

Note: Participants need to complete the devotional lessons for Week 1 prior to the session for Week 1.

Main Point of the Study

When we examine the lives of fierce women in the Bible, we see that they were ordinary women who changed the world by being faithful and obedient. In fact, fierce women such as these have been changing the world for thousands of years. Many have received little recognition, but they lived fiercely anyway. And we can too!

Key Scripture

All Scripture is inspired by God and is useful to teach us what is true and to make us realize what is wrong in our lives. It corrects us when we are wrong and teaches us to do what is right. God uses it to prepare and equip his people to do every good work. (2 Timothy 3:16-17)

What You Will Need

- *Fierce* DVD and a DVD player
- marker board or chart paper and markers
- stick-on name tags and markers (optional)
- iPod, smartphone, or tablet and portable speaker (optional)

Session Outline

Welcome and Opening Prayer (15 minutes)

To create a warm, welcoming environment as the women are gathering before the session begins, consider lighting one or more candles, providing coffee or other refreshments, playing worship music, or all of these. (Bring an iPod, smartphone, or tablet and a portable speaker if desired.) Be sure to provide name tags if the women do not know one another or you have new participants in your group. Take time to introduce yourselves and fellowship for a while. Then, when you are ready to begin, pray the following prayer or offer your own:

Dear God, thank You for using Your Word to guide, instruct, correct, and shape us so that we are prepared and equipped to be the powerful women You need us to be. Help us to learn to be faithful and obedient women who honor You, Lord. We love You. Amen.

Icebreaker (10 minutes)

Go around the circle two times, inviting the women to share short, "popcorn" responses to one of the following questions each time:

- What do you think of when you hear the word *fierce*?
- How would you describe a fierce woman of God?

Video (5 minutes)

Play the Introductory Session video segment on the DVD.

Group Discussion (25 minutes)

- Read 2 Timothy 3:16-17. When we apply these verses to our study of fierce women in the Bible, what can we hope to gain from digging into their stories?
- Review the list of fierce women we will be exploring in this study. Who are least familiar to you? How are you encouraged to know that even lesser-known women of the Bible were heroines who changed the world?
- What are your hopes for this study? What do you want to gain from it?

Closing Prayer (5 minutes)

Close the session by taking personal prayer requests from group members and leading the group in prayer. As you progress to later weeks in the study, you might encourage members to participate in the closing prayer by praying out loud for one another and the requests given.

Week 1

Shiphrah and Puah

Exodus 1

Leader Prep

Bible Story and Theme Overview

This week we explored the story of Shiphrah and Puah. Shiphrah and Puah were ordinary midwives who were ordered to kill the Hebrew boys they helped to deliver. What sets Puah and Shiphrah apart is that in a dangerous and difficult situation they were courageously faithful. They quietly chose to honor God first in their lives, and in return God blessed them. They were human, which means that they were afraid; but they chose to honor God in the midst of their fear. Their fear of God was greater than their fear of an earthly ruler. And as we saw in our readings this week, God rewarded their faithfulness.

How awesome that God would take two simple midwives and use them in such an incredible way! This is God's specialty—taking ordinary people and using them in extraordinary ways. How does God use ordinary people? It's through fierce obedience and faithfulness. May we, like Puah and Shiphrah, be fiercely courageous and live into the extraordinary callings that God has for us; and then may we enjoy the blessings that He will shower upon us!

Main Point

Shiphrah and Puah were women of quiet strength, fearless determination, and faithful resolve who received great blessings from God for their obedience. With the power of God at work in us, we can follow their lead and be fiercely courageous.

Key Scripture

¹⁵Then Pharaoh, the king of Egypt, gave this order to the Hebrew midwives, Shiphrah and Puah: ¹⁶"When you help the Hebrew women as they give birth, watch as they deliver. If the baby is a boy, kill him; if it is a girl, let her live." ¹⁷But because the midwives feared God, they refused to obey the king's orders. They allowed the boys to live, too. (Exodus 1:15-17)

What You Will Need

- Fierce DVD and a DVD player
- marker board or chart paper and markers
- stick-on name tags and markers (optional)
- iPod, smartphone, or tablet and portable speaker (optional)

Session Outline

Welcome and Opening Prayer (5–10 minutes, depending on session length)

To create a warm, welcoming environment as the women are gathering before the session begins, consider lighting one or more candles, providing coffee or other refreshments, playing worship music, or all of these. (Bring an iPod, smartphone, or tablet and a portable speaker if desired.) Be sure to provide name tags if the women do not know one another or you have new participants in your group. Then, when you are ready to begin, pray the following prayer or offer your own:

Dear God, thank You for the witness of faithful women like Shiphrah and Puah who teach us to be fierce in our obedience to You and in our care for others. Thank You for this time that we can come together with fierce sisters to study the Scriptures and learn from one another. Thank You for Your presence within and among us. Amen.

Icebreaker (5 minutes)

Invite the women to share short, "popcorn" responses to the following question:

- Who are some women in the world today whom you would describe as "fierce"? What about them makes them fierce?

Video (15–20 minutes)

Play the "Getting Started: A Devotional Reflection" video for Week 1 (optional), taking a couple of minutes to focus your hearts and minds on God's Word. Then play the teaching video segment for Week 1. Invite participants to complete the Video Viewer Guide for Week 1 in the participant workbook as they watch (page 40).

Group Discussion (25–35 minutes, depending on session length)

Note: More material is provided than you will have time to include. Before the session, select what you want to cover, putting a check mark beside it in your book. Page references are provided for questions related to questions or activities in the participant workbook. For these questions, invite participants to share the answers they wrote in their books.

Video Discussion Questions

- What did you hear about the recurring instruction in Scripture, "Do not be afraid"? Why do you think we see that instruction over and over again throughout the Bible?
- Do you consider yourself "fierce"? Why or why not?
- In what area of your life might you need to find a fierceness in your spirit?

Participant Workbook Discussion Questions

1. [Shiphrah and Puah were ordered to kill all Hebrew babies but] allowed the boys to live! What an act of courage; what fierce faith-fulness to the God they served. Their fear of the Lord and His laws took precedence over what an earthly ruler commanded them to do. Surely, they must have imagined what a king who ordered genocide could have done to them if he came to know his orders had been defied. Surely, they were afraid. But even in their fear, they were faithful. (Day 1, pages 14–15)

- What fears do you face on a reoccurring basis? How have these fears affected your relationship with God? (page 15)
- Read Romans 8:31. What does this verse teach us about facing our fears? (page 16)

2. In my life, the fear of failure and criticism has at times paralyzed me. It's like a snake (which I hate) slithering in front of me, keeping me from taking the next step. These fears of human rejection have, at times, kept me from following Jesus closely, stealing the joy and peace that come from doing life in God's will. (Day 1, page 16)

- What fear has paralyzed you in the past? (page 16)
- What fear has been most destructive in your life? (page 16)
- What does Romans 8:31 teach us about facing our fears? (page 16)

3. There is something ironically beautiful about a feminine warrior—someone who can be soft and strong, gentle and ferocious. (Day 2, page 21)

- Read Proverbs 29:25. How has human opinion influenced you recently? (page 21)
- How does trusting God protect you from the impact of other people's opinions? (page 21)
- Who are some women in your life who could be described as soft and strong, gentle and ferocious?

4. Fierce women have a strength that comes from beyond themselves. They are bathed in the forgiveness and love of Jesus. He holds their hearts so firmly that they are able to find joy and peace in the midst of their battles. These women find their identity in Christ, which provides them with a courage and fortitude that outweighs the fears they face. Fierce women of God are warriors at heart—not savage or violent but tempered with loving-kindness. They are beautiful servants with backbones made of steel. They are wise, gentle, and dangerous—in the best sense of those words. (Day 2, page 21)

- Read Exodus 1:17. According to this verse, why did Shiphrah and Puah refuse to obey the king? (page 22)
- What do you think the king would have done if their plot had been uncovered?
- Review the six steps to help face fears with courage on pages 22–23. How could these steps help you find fierceness when you need it?

5. We truly love others when we put aside our own needs and fears and stand for those who cannot stand for themselves. (Day 3, page 29)

- Read Matthew 22:37-39; John 13:34; and 1 John 3:18. What are the common threads in these verses?
- What does it mean to say that love is a decision?
- Who are the women in your life who put aside their own needs and fears on your behalf (or have done this in the past)?

6. There is evil in our world. But as God's girls we have the opportunity to bring light into the darkness. (Day 3, page 29)

- What are some modern-day evils in our world today?
- What are some ways you can bring light into that darkness?
- What is our responsibility as Christ followers to respond to the injustices in our world? How has God prompted you to take action? (page 28)

7. There is a time to submit, and there is a time to stand. When God's law is clearly violated, as is the case here with a command to murder infants, we cannot pretend we have no responsibility. (Day 4, page 32)

- Read Hebrews 13:17 and Romans 13:1. How do you react to these verses? Would you say you are more of a rule follower or a rule breaker?
- Read Exodus 1:17. How does this verse illustrate Puah's and Shiphrah's respect for God's law? How does our respect or disrespect for God influence our daily decisions? (page 32)
- What are some circumstances when God's law might overrule civic law?

8. It would be naive to think that there may not be consequences when we take a stand. Peter faced hardships, just as Paul, James, and even Jesus did. But they chose to stand anyway. When faced with difficulties, it is good to remember who is our true enemy. (Day 4, page 33)

- Read Acts 5:12-42. What lessons do you extract from this confrontation between the apostles and the Jewish leaders? How might history be different if Peter and the other apostles had complied with the Sanhedrin's order to never again teach in Jesus' name? (pages 32–33)
- How might history be different if Shiphrah and Puah had complied with Pharaoh's edict? (page 33)
- Read Ephesians 6:11. Who is our true enemy? Now read Ephesians 6:10-18. How does the armor of God fit us for battle? (pages 33–34)

9. Heroines in the form of midwives are unexpected. But isn't that just like God? He masters in turning what may seem ordinary to us into the extraordinary when under His control. (Day 5, page 36)

- What about Shiphrah and Puah make them unexpected heroines?
- Who are some other unexpected heroines in the Bible?
- Read Exodus 1:20-21. As you look at your life story, what have been the times when you could say, ". . . so God was good to me"? In other words, when have you experienced God's favor?

10. What sets Puah and Shiphrah apart is that in a dangerous and difficult situation they were courageously faithful. They quietly chose to honor God first in their lives, and in return God blessed them. (Day 5, page 38)

- What temptations to compromise do we face as Christians today? When have you experienced a conflict of your values, and how did you respond? (page 37)
- Read 1 Peter 3:13-17. What practical steps can you take to live above reproach in order to keep your conscience clear? (page 37)
- Read Galatians 6:9. How does this verse encourage you to follow in Shiphrah and Puah's fierce footsteps?

11. Isn't it awesome that God would take two simple midwives and use them in such an incredible way? This is God's specialty—taking ordinary people and using them in extraordinary ways. (Day 5, page 38)

- What thoughts or discoveries are sticking with you from this week's study?

Deeper Conversation (15 minutes)

Divide into smaller groups of two or three for deeper conversation. (Encourage the women to break into different groups each week.) Before the session, write on a marker board or chart paper the question or questions you want the groups to discuss:

- Reflecting on the story of Shiphrah and Puah, what would you say is the relationship between our obedience and God's faithfulness? What are some other stories in the Scriptures that help us understand obedience and faithfulness?
- In what ways are you experiencing some fierceness rising up in your spirit after studying Shiphrah and Puah?

Give a two-minute warning before time is up so that the groups may wrap up their discussion.

Closing Prayer (5 minutes)

Close the session by taking personal prayer requests from group members and leading the group in prayer. As you progress to later weeks in the study, you might encourage members to participate in the closing prayer by praying out loud for one another and the requests given.

Week 2

Deborah

Judges 4–5

Leader Prep

Bible Story and Theme Overview

This week we explored the story of another unlikely heroine, Deborah. At a time when women held little value by the world's standards, Deborah was used by God in mighty ways. She would hold court, perhaps much the way that Moses did, to hear the people's concerns and make righteous decisions. She did this under a palm tree that came to be known as the Palm of Deborah. The entire nation would look to her to settle their disputes. Deborah not only led as a woman of God; she led successfully. God gave her victory in battle as she followed His instructions closely. Because she stayed close to the Lord, not allowing fear and pride to skew her leadership, she followed God's directions closely and gave Him the praise for all success. This was the key to how she juggled her responsibilities—with humility and faithfulness.

Main Point

When someone in power puts aside his or her own agenda to care for those who can't or won't care for themselves, it is love. And it is what we are called to offer those around us.

Key Scripture

⁴Deborah, the wife of Lappidoth, was a prophet who was judging Israel at that time. ⁵She would sit under the Palm of Deborah, between Ramah and Bethel in the hill country of Ephraim, and the Israelites would go to her for judgment. ⁶One day she sent for Barak son of Abinoam, who lived in Kedesh in the land of Naphtali. She said to him, "This is what the LORD, *the God of Israel, commands you: Call out 10,000 warriors from the tribes of Naphtali and Zebulun at Mount Tabor.* ⁷*And I will call out Sisera, commander of Jabin's army, along with his chariots and warriors, to the Kishon River. There I will give you victory over him."*

⁸*Barak told her, "I will go, but only if you go with me."*

⁹*"Very well," she replied, "I will go with you. But you will receive no honor in this venture, for the* LORD's *victory over Sisera will be at the hands of a woman." So Deborah went with Barak to Kedesh.* ¹⁰*At Kedesh, Barak called together the tribes of Zebulun and Naphtali, and 10,000 warriors went up with him. Deborah also went with him.* (Judges 4:4-10)

What You Will Need

- *Fierce* DVD and a DVD player
- marker board or chart paper and markers
- stick-on name tags and markers (optional)
- iPod, smartphone, or tablet and portable speaker (optional)

Session Outline

Welcome and Opening Prayer (5–10 minutes, depending on session length)

To create a warm, welcoming environment as the women are gathering before the session begins, consider lighting one or more candles, providing coffee or other refreshments, playing worship music, or all of these. (Bring an iPod, smartphone, or tablet and a portable speaker if desired.) Be sure to provide name tags if the women do not know one another or you have new participants in your group. Then, when you are ready to begin, pray the following prayer or offer your own:

Dear God, thank You for the witness of Deborah who shows us how to lead with strength and humility. Help us to learn from her how to be a fierce woman of faith. Speak to us now as we study the Scriptures and fellowship together. Amen.

Icebreaker (5 minutes)

Invite the women to share short, "popcorn" responses to the following question:

- Who is a woman in your life who has taught you about tenacity?

Video (15–20 minutes)

Play the "Getting Started: A Devotional Reflection" video for Week 2 (optional), taking a couple of minutes to focus your hearts and minds on God's Word. Then play the teaching video segment for Week 2. Invite participants to complete the Video Viewer Guide for Week 2 in the participant workbook as they watch (page 73).

Group Discussion (25–35 minutes, depending on session length)

Note: More material is provided than you will have time to include. Before the session, select what you want to cover, putting a check mark beside it in your book. Page references are provided for questions related to questions or activities in the participant workbook. For these questions, invite participants to share the answers they wrote in their books.

Video Discussion Questions

- Deborah talked with God and handed down judgments from one spot, under her palm tree. Do you have a special place where you meet with God? What makes it special?
- Deborah learned to encourage herself in the Lord. What does that mean? Have you ever had to give yourself a pep talk to remember to be strong in the Lord?
- When have "what-ifs" kept you from following God's call?

Participant Workbook Discussion Questions

1. We all need people around us to help keep our compass pointed toward True North. It is so easy to become distracted with the busy-ness of life, our own agendas, or even sin. When that happens, we can easily spend months—or even years—headed in the wrong direction. Then one day we wake up to a life filled with strife and wonder, *God where are You?* (Day 1, page 47)

- What did you learn this week about the generations of Israelites that followed after Moses and Joshua? How was Deborah's role as judge like a compass for the Hebrew people?
- Read Judges 4:1-10. When have you cried out to God in distress? (page 46)
- Who has offered godly guidance in your life in the way that Deborah did for the Israelites? (page 46)

2. Part of the process of being made right with God is repentance—the choice to turn away from the sin that has separated us from God. Israel needed to repent for falling away from God repeatedly, and so do we. (Day 1, page 48)

- How do you know when you have drifted away from God? Read Hebrews 2:1 and James 4:8. What can keep us from drifting—or help us once we have drifted—from God's presence? (page 47)
- Read Jeremiah 29:13; Acts 16:31; and John 3:16. What do these verses tell us about seeking and finding God?
- Read James 4:8 and 1 John 1:9. How does repentance make us right with God again? What is our part, and what is God's?

3. After twenty years of oppression from the Canaanites, the people of God cried out to Him for help. As they turned from their wickedness and again sought the Lord, God answered their prayers and led them through Deborah. She had already earned their trust as a judge, mediating their disputes, and now she brought them God's instructions for how to conquer their enemy. (Day 2, page 51)

- Read Judges 5, known as "the song of Deborah." How was this battle won? (page 52)
- Read 1 Samuel 17:47. How is this verse similar to Deborah's song? (page 52)
- Though 1 Samuel 17:47 was written about a different circumstance, its truth applies in Deborah's situation also. How does it apply in your own life circumstances? (page 52)

4. Deborah was a fierce follower of God. She was relentless in wanting to honor Him and to see His will done in her life and in her nation. This alone is what qualified her to do the job that no other women before her had held in the history of God's people. Long before other warrior women of God such as Joan of Arc, Deborah was leading in unexpected ways. (Day 2, page 53)

- When have you felt unqualified for a task to which God has called you?
- What do you think makes a great leader?
- Read Isaiah 55:8 and 1 Samuel 16:7. What examples from your own life illustrate the truths of these verses? (pages 53–54)

5. Fierce women of God come in many shapes and sizes. They have different interests, personalities, talents, and giftings. But there are some traits that mature women of God share—they are faithful, patient, wise, kind, humble, and just. (Day 3, page 58)

- Read Galatians 5:13-26. What attributes or fruit does Paul say will be evident in the life of someone controlled by God's Spirit? (page 57)
- Read Proverbs 31:10-31. How might we describe the depiction of a virtuous woman today? (page 58)
- What aspects of your personality contribute to your fierceness? What traits has God impressed into your DNA that make you just the right person for the life God has called you to?

6. Deborah's qualifications for leadership were her character and her calling. And that is enough by God's standards. When we maintain godly character and lean into the calling God has placed on our lives, we are able to partner with Him to do fierce things. (Day 3, page 60)

- What are the five attributes that serve us in our quest to become fierce women of God? (See pages 59–60.) How can you seek these attributes in your life?
- What helps you to follow God closely? (page 60)
- What keeps you from following God closely? (page 60)

7. God promises us that the weight He intends for us to carry is not only manageable but also light. So if your load is heavy, perhaps you are carrying a load God never intended for you to have. (Day 4, page 65)

- Do you feel you have a healthy, productive rhythm in your life at this point? What feels right and healthy? What feels burdensome or out of balance? (page 64)
- Read Matthew 6:33. How can this word from Jesus help guide your time—your thoughts and actions? (page 65)
- When have you been in a season of exhaustion or burnout? How did you get to that point? How did you get past it?

8. We know that Deborah was a wife, a war strategist, a prophetess, a judge and mediator, and a guide for an entire nation. These are no small roles. But we've also seen that Deborah knew when to seek the help of others in order to balance the responsibilities of her life. Because she stayed close to the Lord, not allowing fear and pride to skew her leadership, she followed God's directions closely and gave Him the praise for all success. This was the key to how she juggled her responsibilities—with humility and faithfulness. (Day 4, page 65)

- What are the various roles you play in your day-to-day life?
- How are you able to stay close to the Lord, even having a busy schedule and wearing many hats?
- How can humility and faithfulness be the key to success in our busy seasons?

9. Strength under the Holy Spirit's direction looks good on Christ followers. It allows us to be strong and to serve, lead well, and still show kindness. A woman who has surrendered her heart, attitudes, and actions to God can live with a fierce sense of purpose, unconcerned with what others think or what roles they think they are supposed to fit into. (Day 5, page 69)

- Who is a woman you know who exhibits humble leadership? (page 69)
- In what ways are you a leader in your family, workplace, community, or church, or all of these?
- What do you think it means to lead with strength?

10. [Deborah] certainly did not fit the stereotypes of her time. . . . She was in the distinct minority in her role as a military, political, and religious leader. Yet she led with strength and wisdom. She sought the help of others and gave them credit for their contributions. Her directions were clear and strong, but they came straight from the Lord; so when the battle was completed, it was to God alone that she sang her praises. (Day 5, page 69)

- Read the victory song of Deborah found in Judges 5. How does she praise God for what has been accomplished? To whom else does she give credit? (page 69)
- It is a sign of maturity and humility to be able to celebrate the successes of others the way Deborah does with Jael and Barak in Judges 5. How can you help others celebrate the victories in their lives? (page 70)
- In your victories and accomplishments, how can you privately and publicly give God the glory? (page 70)

11. When someone in power puts aside their own agenda to care for those who can't or won't care for themselves, it is love. And it is what we are called to offer those around us. (Day 5, page 71)

- What thoughts or discoveries are sticking with you from this week's study?

Deeper Conversation (15 minutes)

Divide into smaller groups of two or three for deeper conversation. (Encourage the women to break into different groups each week.) Before the session, write on a marker board or chart paper the question or questions you want the groups to discuss:

- Leading with strength can be a struggle for us as women trying to follow God closely and be effective in ministry. In wanting to make a difference in the world, we sometimes feel the tension of being both gentle and decisive, feminine and fierce. We don't want to be labeled as too aggressive, but we do want to get things done. Can the two truly coexist? Share your thoughts and discuss the struggle of being a woman in leadership today. How can women support one another and cheer one another on?
- Review the common characteristics of fierce women on Day 5 (page 70). What would you add to the list? How have you seen these characteristics lived out among women you know—or maybe even in your own leadership?

Closing Prayer (5 minutes)

Close the session by taking personal prayer requests from group members and leading the group in prayer. As you progress to later weeks in the study, you might encourage members to participate in the Closing Prayer by praying out loud for one another and the requests given.

Week 3

Naaman's Slave Girl

2 Kings 5

Leader Prep

Bible Story and Theme Overview

This week's heroine doesn't get name recognition in Scripture. In fact, very little is written about her at all. There are only two verses dedicated to her, yet from those verses we see great character. She is a child who was ripped from her parents during a time of war. She was taken to a new country, a new home—one with a different religion, customs, and expectations. Most likely she was sold at the slave market in Damascus. She served as a maid to the wife of one of Aram's greatest commanders, Naaman. Naaman had the deadly disease of leprosy, a skin disease that had no cure and was highly contagious. This is where our young maiden speaks up and her fierce faith shines through. This young Israelite has compassion on her master and offers her best advice: take him to see the prophet of God in Israel, Elisha. She knows that even in a foreign land the power of God is at work, and she is willing to share this with those who have captured her.

Main Point

Fierce women of God know that their identities are wrapped up in their relationship with Christ and not the approval of others, and that is freeing. It frees us to give others what they simply do not deserve. In return, we need no credit or accolades because the act of generosity is enough.

Key Scripture

[1]The king of Aram had great admiration for Naaman, the commander of his army, because through him the LORD had given Aram great victories. But though Naaman was a mighty warrior, he suffered from leprosy.

[2]At this time Aramean raiders had invaded the land of Israel, and among their captives was a young girl who had been given to Naaman's wife as a maid. [3]One day the girl said to her mistress, "I wish my master would go to see the prophet in Samaria. He would heal him of his leprosy."

[4]So Naaman told the king what the young girl from Israel had said. [5]"Go and visit the prophet," the king of Aram told him. "I will send a letter of introduction for you to take to the king of Israel." So Naaman started out, carrying as gifts 750 pounds of silver, 150 pounds of gold, and ten sets of clothing. [6]The letter to the king of Israel said: "With this letter I present my servant Naaman. I want you to heal him of his leprosy."

[7]When the king of Israel read the letter, he tore his clothes in dismay and said, "Am I God, that I can give life and take it away? Why is this man asking me to heal someone with leprosy? I can see that he's just trying to pick a fight with me."

[8]But when Elisha, the man of God, heard that the king of Israel had torn his clothes in dismay, he sent this message to him: "Why are you so upset? Send Naaman to me, and he will learn that there is a true prophet here in Israel."

[9]So Naaman went with his horses and chariots and waited at the door of Elisha's house.

(2 Kings 5:1-9)

What You Will Need

- *Fierce* DVD and a DVD player
- marker board or chart paper and markers
- stick-on name tags and markers (optional)
- iPod, smartphone, or tablet and portable speaker (optional)

Session Outline

Welcome and Opening Prayer (5–10 minutes, depending on session length)

To create a warm, welcoming environment as the women are gathering before the session begins, consider lighting one or more candles, providing coffee or other refreshments, playing worship music, or all of these. (Bring an iPod, smartphone, or tablet and a portable speaker if desired.) Be sure to provide name tags if the women do not know one another or you have new participants in your group. Then, when you are ready to begin, pray the following prayer or offer your own:

Dear God, thank you for the witness of this young servant girl who shows us how to do what's right when we don't have to. We ask You to fill us with that same courage. Amen.

Icebreaker (5 minutes)

Invite the women to share short, "popcorn" responses to the following question:

- Who are some minor characters in your story who have made a big impact by doing what is right?

Video (15–20 minutes)

Play the "Getting Started: A Devotional Reflection" video for Week 3 (optional), taking a couple of minutes to focus your hearts and minds on God's Word. Then play the teaching video segment for Week 3. Invite participants to complete the Video Viewer Guide for Week 3 in the participant workbook as they watch (pages 102–103).

Group Discussion (25–35 minutes, depending on session length)

Note: More material is provided than you will have time to include. Before the session, select what you want to cover, putting a check mark beside it in your book. Page references are provided for questions related to questions or activities in the participant workbook. For these questions, invite participants to share the answers they wrote in their books.

Video Discussion Questions

- When have you had a chance to offer kindness to someone who has been unkind to you?
- Why should you offer hope and healing to someone who has inflicted pain on you and those you love?
- Has your kindness led another person to worship God? Tell about that experience.

Participant Workbook Discussion Questions

1. I am struck with [the young girl's] fierce faith in a difficult situation. She is a child slave. She has been snatched from her home. Sold! Surely at some point she had to ask, "God, where are you? Why haven't you rescued me? Where is my mom? God, don't you care?" Surely, she must have felt angry, sad, scared, and confused. But what we see in this brief encounter is a rock-solid faith in God. This little girl knows that despite her own situation, God is able. (Day 1, page 77)

   - How is it that two people can go through similar situations and come out in such different places? (page 77)

- When you experience difficulties in life, how do you typically respond? (page 78)
- How has your relationship with God been impacted in difficult seasons? (page 78)

2. When asked by His disciples, "Who is the greatest in the Kingdom of Heaven?" Jesus responds by inviting a child to come and be with them. This child is the object lesson for the disciples. Jesus holds up this child who, in that culture, had no rights and no voice, and says that the one who takes on the same position—innocent and child-like—is great in the eyes of heaven. Childlike faith is not weak; it is pure and strong. (Day 1, page 78)

- Read Matthew 18:2-4. What do Jesus' words teach us about faith? (page 78)
- How does Naaman's slave girl teach us about what it means to be the greatest in the kingdom of heaven?
- In what ways is childlike faith a demonstration of strength?

3. I will never forget [the prison inmate's] words, "It's time I learned to thrive in my Babylon." I thought of people suffering with diseases such as cystic fibrosis, cerebral palsy, and cancer as well as addiction, depression, and bipolar disorder. I thought of friends who were going through unwanted divorce, those who had lost a child or spouse too soon in life, and people going through financial distress—all who felt lonely and perhaps even unloved. . . .
   Sometimes we find ourselves living in Babylon through our own poor decisions. But sometimes life just happens. Disease, financial crises, and broken relationships are, unfortunately, part of the human condition—the result of a world marred by sin and brokenness. It is in these times that we have the choice to turn from God or run to Him. (Day 2, page 81)

- What Babylons have you experienced? Did you survive or thrive during those times? (page 81)
- Read Psalm 34:18. How can this verse help you as you travel through dark times? (page 81)
- What would you say is the difference between surviving and thriving?

4. Despite the fact that she is living as a slave in a foreign land, this girl demonstrates confident faith in the power of God to work through his prophet Elisha to heal her master's leprosy. In her own distress she has not given up on God. That is a powerful lesson for us. We can have this confidence as well, depending not only on God's power but also on the promises of Jesus. (Day 2, page 83)

- How have your struggles affected your relationship with God? (page 83)
- What testimonies of God's faithfulness during difficult times do you have that could encourage others? (page 84)
- Read John 16:33 and Romans 8:38-39. What are the promises contained in these verses? (page 83) How do these promises encourage us to trust in God's faithfulness?

5. Disease, betrayal, crime, violence, oppression, addiction, even slavery are daily battles that many people face. One day God will set things right. In the meantime, we have to figure out how to live like Christ even in our pain. (Day 3, pages 85–86)

- When and how have you experienced the brokenness of this planet? (page 86)
- Read 2 Peter 3:9. What does this verse teach us about God's plan? (page 86)
- Read 2 Corinthians 12:9a. What did the apostle Paul say about grace? How would you define grace in your own words? (page 86)

6. When we pray in a crisis, God will respond to us in one of two ways. He will either remove the source of pain, or He will give us the strength to go through it. (Day 3, page 86)

- When have you experienced a time of God either removing pain or giving you strength to go through it? Share about that experience.
- When life treats you unfairly, do you tend to blame God or run to God? Why do you think you respond that way?
- Read Hebrews 12:15. What does Paul say can happen if we don't respond to God's grace? (page 87) How is grace the antidote to whatever pain you're facing?

7. Reluctantly, Naaman does as Elisha instructs him to do, and his leprosy is miraculously healed. But something even more significant happens.

This powerful military leader who has great favor with the enemy king of Aram comes to know the awesome power of the God of his enemy—the one true God. Through this experience he comes to a faith of his own. Imagine the implications this had for a man of his influence. I like to imagine that Naaman returned and sought out our little servant girl to thank her and talk with her about her amazing God. (Day 4, page 92)

- Read 2 Kings 5:4-14. What did the king tell Naaman to do, and what was his response? What did Elisha tell Naaman to do, and what was his initial response? How did Naaman's officers convince him to do as Elisha instructed? (page 92)
- Read 2 Kings 5:15. What does Naaman come to know? (page 92)
- What do you guess are the implications of Naaman coming to know the one true God?

8. Through our faith and courage, God is able to use us in very difficult situations. (Day 4, page 95)

- Read Isaiah 61:3. How have you seen God bring something beautiful out of hard situations? (page 94)
- In what unique circumstances might God want to use *you* to shine His light? (page 94)
- Read Galatians 6:10. What are we to do and when? (page 94)

9. Fierce women of God know that their identities are wrapped up in their relationship with Christ and not the approval of others, and that is freeing. It frees us to give others what they simply do not deserve. In return, we need no credit or accolades because the act of generosity is enough. (Day 5, page 98)

- Would you say that you are free from the need to gain the approval of others? Why or why not?
- How might others benefit if you began to err on the side of generosity? (page 98)
- How does doing the right thing in difficult circumstances set us apart?

10. This little girl errs on the side of generosity in an unwelcome and painful situation. That is amazing. Equally amazing is that God heals this pagan commander of an enemy army. This little girl points Naaman to the prophet Elisha; and Elisha, through the power of

God, heals him! This is a man who has led raids against Elisha's own people—God's chosen people! Yet God loves Naaman and shows him mercy. (Day 5, page 99)

- Read Luke 4:14-30. What does this passage teach us about faith and miracles? (page 99)
- Look again at verses 25-26. When there was a famine in the land, where was Elijah sent to minister—and to whom? (page 99)
- What is significant about Elijah, Elisha, and our young heroine extending grace and love to foreigners?

11. Doing the right thing in difficult circumstances is hard. But it's one of the things that sets those with a fierce faith apart from the pack. Forgiving when the wound is deep, sharing our faith when it feels awkward, and slowing down to make time for others are all ways of being generous with those around us. (Day 5, page 97)

- What thoughts or discoveries are sticking with you from this week's study?

Deeper Conversation (15 minutes)

Divide into smaller groups of two or three for deeper conversation. (Encourage the women to break into different groups each week.) Before the session, write on a marker board or chart paper the question or questions you want the groups to discuss:

- Fierce women of God are free to be generous with grace, love, and kindness. Are you free? If not, what holds you captive? (Is it anger, addiction, depression, insecurity, loneliness, fear?) (page 98)
- How might [whatever is holding you captive] be impacting your testimony? (page 98)

Give a two-minute warning before time is up so that the groups may wrap up their discussion.

Closing Prayer (5 minutes)

Close the session by taking personal prayer requests from group members and leading the group in prayer. Encourage members to participate in the closing prayer by praying out loud for one another and the requests given.

Week 4

The Samaritan Woman

John 4

Leader Prep

Bible Story and Theme Overview

This week we explored the story of a Samaritan woman. In the heat of the day, Jesus meets a woman of Samaria at a well and does something shocking. He speaks to her. A Jewish man speaking to a Samaritan—especially a woman—is just not done. But Jesus breaks that barrier and asks her for a drink of water. It is a simple request that begins an honest dialogue and ultimately leads her to faith in Jesus. She has been married five times and is now living with another man—not to mention the fact that she's a woman, having little worth in society's eyes. It would be rare for a man to address a woman in public, especially a woman of her standing in life. But Jesus is not concerned with what others are thinking. His concentration is on restoring her into a right relationship with God. Jesus shows love for her—real love that speaks the hard truths and then comes alongside to bring restoration and wholeness.

Main Point

Sharing the love of God is not just a responsibility we have as followers of Christ; it is a privilege. We are called to reach out to messy people, inviting them into our homes and churches and offering them genuine love.

Key Scriptures

¹Jesus knew the Pharisees had heard that he was baptizing and making more disciples than John ²(though Jesus himself didn't baptize them—his disciples did). ³So he left Judea and returned to Galilee.

⁴He had to go through Samaria on the way. ⁵Eventually he came to the Samaritan village of Sychar, near the field that Jacob gave to his son Joseph. ⁶Jacob's well was there; and Jesus, tired from the long walk, sat wearily beside the well about noontime. ⁷Soon a Samaritan woman came to draw water, and Jesus said to her, "Please give me a drink." ⁸He was alone at the time because his disciples had gone into the village to buy some food.

⁹The woman was surprised, for Jews refuse to have anything to do with Samaritans. She said to Jesus, "You are a Jew, and I am a Samaritan woman. Why are you asking me for a drink?"

¹⁰Jesus replied, "If you only knew the gift God has for you and who you are speaking to, you would ask me, and I would give you living water."

¹¹"But sir, you don't have a rope or a bucket," she said, "and this well is very deep. Where would you get this living water? ¹²And besides, do you think you're greater than our ancestor Jacob, who gave us this well? How can you offer better water than he and his sons and his animals enjoyed?"

¹³Jesus replied, "Anyone who drinks this water will soon become thirsty again. ¹⁴But those who drink the water I give will never be thirsty again. It becomes a fresh, bubbling spring within them, giving them eternal life."

¹⁵"Please, sir," the woman said, "give me this water! Then I'll never be thirsty again, and I won't have to come here to get water."

¹⁶"Go and get your husband," Jesus told her.

¹⁷"I don't have a husband," the woman replied.

Jesus said, "You're right! You don't have a husband— ¹⁸for you have had five husbands, and you aren't even married to the man you're living with now. You certainly spoke the truth!"

¹⁹"Sir," the woman said, "you must be a prophet. ²⁰So tell me, why is it that you Jews insist that Jerusalem is the only place of worship, while we Samaritans claim it is here at Mount Gerizim, where our ancestors worshiped?"

²¹Jesus replied, "Believe me, dear woman, the time is coming when it will no longer matter whether you worship the Father on this mountain or in Jerusalem. ²²You Samaritans know very little about the one you worship, while we Jews know all about him, for salvation comes through the Jews. ²³But the time is coming—indeed it's here now—when true worshipers will worship the Father in spirit and in truth. The Father is looking for those who will worship him that way. ²⁴For God is Spirit, so those who worship him must worship in spirit and in truth."

²⁵The woman said, "I know the Messiah is coming—the one who is called Christ. When he comes, he will explain everything to us."

²⁶Then Jesus told her, "I AM the Messiah!" (John 4:1-26)

What You Will Need

- Fierce DVD and a DVD player
- marker board or chart paper and markers
- stick-on name tags and markers (optional)
- iPod, smartphone, or tablet and portable speaker (optional)

Session Outline

Welcome and Opening Prayer (5–10 minutes, depending on session length)

To create a warm, welcoming environment as the women are gathering before the session begins, consider lighting one or more candles, providing coffee or other refreshments, playing worship music, or all of these. (Bring an iPod, smartphone, or tablet and a portable speaker if desired.) Be sure to provide name tags if the women do not know one another or you have new participants in your group. Then, when you are ready to begin, pray the following prayer or offer your own:

Dear God, thank You for the story of a Samaritan woman who shows us that no matter who we are, where we've been, or what we've done, we are never outside the love and grace of God. Speak to us as we study Your Word and fellowship together. Amen.

Icebreaker (5 minutes)

Invite the women to share short, "popcorn" responses to the following question:

• When have you broken or overcome a barrier to show someone love?

Video (15–20 minutes)

Play the "Getting Started: A Devotional Reflection" video for Week 4 (optional), taking a couple of minutes to focus your hearts and minds on God's Word. Then play the teaching video segment for Week 4. Invite participants to complete the Video Viewer Guide for Week 4 in the participant workbook as they watch (page 137).

Group Discussion (25–35 minutes, depending on session length)

Note: More material is provided than you will have time to include. Before the session, select what you want to cover, putting a check mark beside it in your book. Page references are provided for questions related to questions or activities in the participant workbook. For these questions, invite participants to share the answers they wrote in their books.

Video Discussion Questions

• When has God positioned Himself for a unique encounter with you?
• When have you had a personal encounter with Jesus? What was that experience like?
• What do you think it means to have a rich and satisfying life?

Participant Workbook Discussion Questions

(1.) The text says, "He had to go through Samaria." Geographically speaking, this isn't true. There are other routes to be taken from Judea in the south to Galilee in the north. But Jesus ventures west to go through Samaria. He doesn't head up the flat ground of Jordan in the river valley but traverses the mountains to go through Samaria on his way to the sea. (Day 1, pages 108–109)

- What is significant about Jesus taking that journey through Samaria?
- What is significant about the place, the time of day, and the woman he meets in Samaria?
- Read John 4:16-17. What does Jesus reveal about her past and current living situation? (page 110)
- Read John 4:27. How do the disciples respond when they return to find Jesus talking with the woman at the well? (page 110) What is the reason for their reaction? What does this say to us about Jesus?

Shocked –

2. Jesus is not concerned with what others are thinking. His concentration is on restoring [the Samaritan woman] into a right relationship with God. Jesus shows love for her—real love that speaks the hard truths and then comes alongside to bring restoration and wholeness. Perhaps Jesus "had to go through Samaria" because this encounter was so important, so desperately needed, for this woman—and for you and me. (Day 1, page 111)

- Read John 3:16-17. Whom does God so love, and what did God's love prompt Him to do? (page 111)
- How have you felt God go out of His way to show you love in the past? (page 111)
- Do you ever feel concerned about what others are thinking when you show love to those who might be considered outcasts in society? Share about your struggle to show love without caring what others think.

3. Sometimes we get respect confused with acceptance. Respect does not necessitate agreeing with everything a person says or does. It certainly doesn't mean we put a stamp of approval on sinful behavior. It does, however, involve treating every person with dignity and love. Jesus is polite in this encounter. He deals with [the Samaritan woman] directly, honestly, and kindly; and as a result, this inter-

action is effective in changing her life—and ultimately the lives of many others. (Day 2, page 114)

- What do you think is the difference between respect and acceptance? Or is there any difference?
- Direct, honest, and kind—which of these three do you leave out most often in your interactions with others? (page 115)
- How could it improve your life (and the lives of those around you) if you incorporated a balance of the three? (page 115)

4. Sharing the love of God is not just a responsibility we have as followers of Christ; it is a privilege. We are called to reach out to messy people, inviting them into our homes and churches and offering them genuine love. So, taking the time to think through the specifics of how we interact and how we handle conversations—especially difficult and important ones—is critical. Being intentional about the where, when, and how will make you more effective and convincing as you live into your call as a Christ follower. (Day 2, page 116)

- Why do details and intentionality matter as we share the love of God?
- Where might you position yourself in the way that Jesus positioned Himself at the well? (page 117)
- In what ways is it a privilege to share the love of God?

5. We all thirst for things in life. But so many of the things we thirst for never fully satisfy us. As the desire for these things overtakes our desire for God, we fall into a trap; and it leaves us with a thirst that can never be quenched. Thirsting for things over our desire for God actually has a nasty little name: sin. And sin is addictive. We thirst for something; we crave it. But even when we have it, we aren't satisfied. (Day 3, pages 121–22)

- Read John 4:10-14. Imagine yourself walking up to the well and finding Jesus waiting for you. How would you feel meeting Him face-to-face? Would you have any fears, and if so, what would they be? (page 121)
- What does Jesus say about living water in comparison to the water in the well? (page 121)
- What are you really thirsty for in life? (Consider what consumes your thought life and your time as you answer this question.) (page 121)

6. We often ask, seek, and knock in the all the wrong places. We try to fill our emptiness, to quench our thirst; but without Christ, the emptiness will always return. (Day 3, page 123)

- Read Matthew 7:7. What promises does Jesus make in this verse? (page 123)
- Read these other passages that refer to living water: Zechariah 14:8-9; Revelation 7:13-17; Revelation 21:6-8. How might this living water that the Scriptures describe meet your "thirst"? How might it meet your deepest longing? (pages 122–23)
- Have you ever found yourself asking, seeking, and knocking in the wrong places when Jesus was the answer all along? If so, share about that time.

7. A few phrases I've developed that help me when my nerves try to take control: (1) Get over yourself and just focus on God; (2) Don't fear people; love them. When the Scripture and the power of the cross take center stage, I feel a new sense of purpose. It's not about me; it's about Him. And that helps me find courage and purpose. Loving people who may be judging you, who may be talking about you, who may not like you is hard. But learning to trust God has helped me deal with my fears of judgment and inadequacy as I have shared my faith for decades now. (Day 4, page 126)

- What fears do you have when you feel God's prompting to share your faith—whether with one person or a group? How have you dealt with those fears in the past? (page 127)
- Read 2 Timothy 1:7 and Romans 1:16. What do theses verses teach us? (page 127)
- How do we overcome a spirit of timidity?

8. Our heroine this week likely had some fears about sharing Christ in public settings. With her history of having five marriages and now living with another man, there surely had been many who whispered about her. At other times she probably had wished for whispers when she faced open rebuke in the marketplace. But even so, after her encounter with Jesus she is fiercely emboldened to go and share what she has found despite any fears. So she invites everyone she meets to come and see! (Day 4, page 129)

(•) Who has been there to encourage you in your faith journey? How did they help you to "come and see" who Jesus is? (page 128)

- What fears might be holding you back from your best life? (page 129)
- How can leaning into our fierceness help us overcome our fears?

9. This woman of Samaria has had five marriages and is now involved with another man. We can pass judgment, and surely many did. But then we wonder, *How did the marriages end? Did her husbands die, or was she abandoned?* Either way, we know there has been heartbreak, pain, and perhaps scandal. . . . Surely she must question her worth and purpose. Jesus knows that she comes to the well with a thirst for more than water. She is thirsty for love, belonging, and purpose; and He meets her at this point of need. (Day 5, page 131)

- Read John 4:21, 23-24. What does it mean to worship God with the "right heart"? (page 132)
- What would be different in our world today if we saw others as Jesus saw this fierce Samaritan woman?
- How could considering the backstories of people we encounter help us love them more fully?

10. God is interested in our response to who He is. He longs for us to live our lives as worshipers, not just to attend services of worship. It's not about location or ritual or hymnals, although those things can have meaning. It's about living so that we express our love in pure, sincere, and practical ways. (Day 5, page 133)

- How would you describe a lifestyle of worship? (page 133)
- What practical steps can you take to move toward this lifestyle? (page 133)
- Read Matthew 28:18-20. What does this passage tell us about the next step of true worshipers?

11. Once we encounter Jesus for ourselves, we have the privilege of sharing His love and message with as many people as we can. That's what our fierce woman of Sychar did, and it changed not only her life but also the lives of so many others. (Day 5, page 135)

- What thoughts or discoveries are sticking with you from this week's study?

Deeper Conversation (15 minutes)

Divide into smaller groups of two or three for deeper conversation. (Encourage the women to break into different groups each week.) Before the session, write on a marker board or chart paper the question or questions you want the groups to discuss:

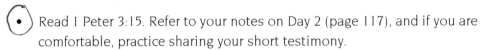 Read 1 Peter 3:15. Refer to your notes on Day 2 (page 117), and if you are comfortable, practice sharing your short testimony.

Give a two-minute warning before time is up so that the groups may wrap up their discussion.

Closing Prayer (5 minutes)

Close the session by taking personal prayer requests from group members and leading the group in prayer. Encourage members to participate in the closing prayer by praying out loud for one another and the requests given.

Week 5

Dorcas

Acts 9

Leader Prep

Bible Story and Theme Overview

This week we explored the story of Dorcas. Like Shiphrah and Puah, we have very little information about the life of Dorcas. The writer of Acts, traditionally thought to be the physician Luke, simply tells us that she was always doing kind things for people, especially those in need. Apparently, a great deal of those acts involved sewing. Dorcas had blessed many by sharing her ability to sew. Her acts of kindness were well known throughout the community; and when she passed away, there was such grief that the apostle Peter was summoned in hopes that she might be resurrected. Dorcas is counted among the heroines of Scripture because through her quiet example we see how we can use our abilities to bless others.

Main Point

We are known by our actions, so live in such a way that your actions speak of a life centered in Christ—that when others hear your name, they think of holiness and godliness.

Key Scriptures

[39]So Peter returned with them; and as soon as he arrived, they took him to the upstairs room. The room was filled with widows who were weeping and showing him the coats and other clothes Dorcas had made for them. [40]But Peter asked them all to leave the room; then he knelt and prayed. Turning to the body he said, "Get up, Tabitha." And she opened her eyes! When she saw Peter, she sat up! [41]He

gave her his hand and helped her up. Then he called in the widows and all the believers, and he presented her to them alive.

⁴²The news spread through the whole town, and many believed in the Lord. (Acts 9:39-42)

What You Will Need

- Fierce DVD and a DVD player
- marker board or chart paper and markers
- stick-on name tags and markers (optional)
- iPod, smartphone, or tablet and portable speaker (optional)

Session Outline

Welcome and Opening Prayer (5–10 minutes, depending on session length)

To create a warm, welcoming environment as the women are gathering before the session begins, consider lighting one or more candles, providing coffee or other refreshments, playing worship music, or all of these. (Bring an iPod, smartphone, or tablet and a portable speaker if desired.) Be sure to provide name tags if the women do not know one another or you have new participants in your group. Then, when you are ready to begin, pray the following prayer or offer your own:

Dear God, You are a God of miracles. Thank You for your amazing love and power at work in our lives. Thank You for the witness of Dorcas and her friends who believed in Your power. Help us to believe. Come and be present as we study Your Word and fellowship together. Amen.

Icebreaker (5 minutes)

Invite the women to share short, "popcorn" responses to the following question:

- What is your most precious homemade garment, blanket, decoration, or toy from any season of your life?

Video (15–20 minutes)

Play the "Getting Started: A Devotional Reflection" video for Week 5 (optional), taking a couple of minutes to focus your hearts and minds on God's Word. Then play the teaching video segment for Week 5. Invite participants to complete the Video Viewer Guide for Week 5 in the participant workbook as they watch (page 168).

Group Discussion (25–35 minutes, depending on session length)

Note: More material is provided than you will have time to include. Before the session, select what you want to cover, putting a check mark beside it in your book. Page references are provided for questions related to questions or activities in the participant workbook. For these questions, invite participants to share the answers they wrote in their books.

Video Discussion Questions

- In your own words, what is the difference between talents, abilities, and spiritual gifts?
- How do our experiences contribute to our ability to share the love of God in the world?
- Why are painful experiences the most powerful in our ministry to others?

Participant Workbook Discussion Questions

1. One of the most precious gifts I have ever received is a tattered quilt. It was tattered when I received it; and after many years of use, it is in barely usable condition. But I love it. . . . One particularly hardened older lady of the community [I served] that I had come to love was Miss Dilly. . . . On my last day of work Miss Dilly brought me a gift— the tattered quilt. . . . The tattered quilt was her way of using the skill she had and the materials at her disposal to show love. And it was precious! (Day 1, pages 139–41)

   Modern Wedding Quilt

   - When has someone blessed you through a simple gift? (page 141)
   - How does that gift differ from other things you have received? (page 141)
   - What is it about handmade gifts that are so special?

2. Dorcas turned her ability to sew into a ministry and blessed many people. Her acts of kindness were well known throughout the community; and when she passed away, there was such grief that the apostle Peter was summoned in hopes that she might be res-urrected. . . . Dorcas is counted among the heroines of Scripture because through her quiet example we see how we can use our abili-ties to bless others. (Day 1, pages 141–42)

   - Read 1 Peter 4:10. What are we instructed to do with our gifts and abili-ties? (page 142)
   - What abilities has God given *you* that you could use to bless others? (page 142)
   - What are some ways God has used your abilities to bless others?

3. Dorcas had a reputation in the community as someone who not only observed but also responded to the needs of those around her in practical ways. Most likely there were those who didn't appreciate what she did at times, but apparently Dorcas was not deterred. She just kept right on serving. (Day 2, page 145)

    • Read Acts 9:36. What does this verse tell us that Dorcas did, and how often did she do it? (page 145)
    • Read Ephesians 2:10. According to this verse, how has God planned that we should spend our lives? (page 145)
    • Read Philippians 2:4; Galatians 6:2; and Romans 12:10. What do these verses have in common? (page 146)

4. Throughout Scripture we read that we are to do life with one another. We are to care for one another, love one another, help one another, and encourage one another. The list goes on and on. God means for us to live in community. As we do this, we're to be sensitive to the needs of those around us. (Day 2, page 146)

    • How have you spent time helping others recently? (page 146)
    • What issues do you see in your community that need to be addressed? (page 146)
    • What national or global concerns tug at your heart? What might you do to make a difference in these areas? (page 147)

5. When we meet Jesus, our names may not change, but what our names stand for surely should. As others observe your life as a follower of Christ, let them see integrity. Let them observe the fruit of the Spirit—love, joy, peace, patience, kindness, goodness, gentleness, faithfulness, and self-control. (Day 3, page 152)

    • Read Matthew 16:17-18. What name does Jesus give Simon? What does Jesus tell Peter He will do? (page 151)
    • When others hear your name, what qualities do you want to come to mind? (page 152)
    • Read Proverbs 22:1. What does it mean to have a good name? (page 152)

6. We are known by our actions, so live in such a way that your actions speak of a life centered in Christ—that when others hear your name, they think of holiness and godliness. (Day 3, page 153)

- Who in your life lives in such a way that her actions speak of a life centered in Christ?
- Who are the women in your community who have a long reputation of serving others?
- What does it take to have a good name and a lasting, revered reputation?

7. As we search the Scriptures, we see that most miracles come at a time of desperation. Someone is hurting. People are in need. Human resources have failed. At that point of desperation, God's power shines. (Day 4, page 156)

- When have you seen God's power shine in desperate situations?
- Read Mark 5:25-34. In what times of your life have you been able to relate to this woman? When have you been desperate to reach Jesus? (pages 156–57)
- What are some other stories you know from the Scriptures about God's power shining in desperate moments?

8. Desperation heightens our prayer life. When a friend or family member gets the dreaded diagnosis, when a child we love is in crisis, or when a marriage or other significant relationship is in trouble, we turn to God. And it's right that we do. But all too often we cry out to God only after we have come to the end of ourselves. When science and medicine have failed us, when we're at the end of our resources, when we can no longer control the situation, we cry out to God. (Day 4, page 160)

- Why do you think we wait until we get to the end of ourselves before we cry out to God?
- Read John 14:12-14. What is the premise and promise contained here? (page 160)
- When and where have you seen God miraculously show up in your life in the past? (page 161)

9. I often hear people say that they don't speak much about their faith because it is just too private. This is not a healthy attitude for us to have as believers. Our faith is a deeply personal experience, but it's not meant to be private. (Day 5, page 165)

- Read Acts 9:40-43. What did the believers of Joppa do after they saw Dorcas alive again? According to verse 42, what is the result of their response? (page 164)

- Read Psalm 107:2. What does this verse call us to do? (page 165)
- Why do you think is it unhealthy for believers to keep their faith private?

10. As God's girls, we have received the miraculous gift of life through God's Son, Jesus. In the same way that many were drawn to Christ by seeing Dorcas alive, we have the opportunity for others to be drawn to Christ by seeing Him alive in us. Let the redeemed of the Lord say so! And as the old saying goes, let us use words if necessary. (Day 5, page 167)

- How has the faith of your friends helped to lead you to faith or healing in Christ? (page 166)
- What does it mean for others to see Christ alive in you?
- How have you seen God work miracles in your life or in those in your community? Do you believe that God can use you to work miracles? Why or why not?

11. As we find the courage to share our faith, we put into action the salvation that we have received. In short, *faithful people share their faith.* (page 165)

- What thoughts or discoveries are sticking with you from this week's study?

Deeper Conversation (15 minutes)

Divide into smaller groups of two or three for deeper conversation. (Encourage the women to break into different groups each week.) Before the session, write on a marker board or chart paper the question or questions you want the groups to discuss:

- What parts of your story might prove encouraging to others? (page 166)
- What specific talents, abilities, or spiritual gifts would you like to lean into in order to be a blessing to others?

Give a two-minute warning before time is up so that the groups may wrap up their discussion.

Closing Prayer (5 minutes)

Close the session by taking personal prayer requests from group members and leading the group in prayer. Encourage members to participate in the closing prayer by praying out loud for one another and the requests given.

Week 6

Lois and Eunice

Acts 16 and 2 Timothy 1

Leader Prep

Bible Story and Theme Overview

This week we explored the story of Eunice and Lois in the New Testament. They were the mother and grandmother of a young man named Timothy. Timothy's dad was a Greek and, therefore, probably not a believer. But his mother and grandmother, Eunice and Lois, were Jews, and they had come to know and love Christ as their Savior. These women were intentional in passing along to Timothy a rich heritage of faith. Timothy plays a significant role in the New Testament, but we probably never would have known of him if it weren't for these two very special ladies who were intentional in helping him develop his faith.

Main Point

Whether we realize it or not, we are constantly influencing others. Let's live with purpose and intentionally choose language, habits, attitudes, and actions that reflect those of Christ.

Key Scriptures

¹Paul came to Derbe and then to Lystra, where a disciple named Timothy lived, whose mother was Jewish and a believer but whose father was a Greek. ²The believers at Lystra and Iconium spoke well of him. ³Paul wanted to take him along on the journey, so he circumcised him because of the Jews who lived in that area, for they all knew that his father was a Greek. (Acts 16:1-3 NIV)

¹*Paul, an apostle of Christ Jesus by the will of God, in keeping with the promise of life that is in Christ Jesus,*

²*To Timothy, my dear son:*

Grace, mercy and peace from God the Father and Christ Jesus our Lord.

³*I thank God, whom I serve, as my ancestors did, with a clear conscience, as night and day I constantly remember you in my prayers.* ⁴*Recalling your tears, I long to see you, so that I may be filled with joy.* ⁵*I am reminded of your sincere faith, which first lived in your grandmother Lois and in your mother Eunice and, I am persuaded, now lives in you also.* (2 Timothy 1:1-5 NIV)

What You Will Need

- *Fierce* DVD and a DVD player
- marker board or chart paper and markers
- stick-on name tags and markers (optional)
- iPod, smartphone, or tablet and portable speaker (optional)

Session Outline

Welcome and Opening Prayer (5–10 minutes, depending on session length)

To create a warm, welcoming environment as the women are gathering before the session begins, consider lighting one or more candles, providing coffee or other refreshments, playing worship music, or all of these. (Bring an iPod, smartphone, or tablet and a portable speaker if desired.) Be sure to provide name tags if the women do not know one another or you have new participants in your group. Then, when you are ready to begin, pray the following prayer or offer your own:

Dear God, thank You for the story of Lois and Eunice. Thank You for all the women in our own lives who have lovingly pointed us to You. Come and be present as we study Your Word and fellowship together. Amen.

Icebreaker (5 minutes)

Invite the women to share short, "popcorn" responses to the following question:

- What wise lesson from a woman in your family—whether your mother, grandmother, favorite aunt, or someone else—sticks with you to this day?

Video (15–20 minutes)

Play the "Getting Started: A Devotional Reflection" video for Week 6 (optional), taking a couple of minutes to focus your hearts and minds on God's Word. Then play the teaching video segment for Week 6. Invite participants to complete the Video Viewer Guide for Week 6 in the participant workbook as they watch (page 202).

Group Discussion (25–35 minutes, depending on session length)

Note: More material is provided than you will have time to include. Before the session, select what you want to cover, putting a check mark beside it in your book. Page references are provided for questions related to questions or activities in the participant workbook. For these questions, invite participants to share the answers they wrote in their books.

Video Discussion Questions

- Why is it so important to model behavior we want others to emulate?
- Who are some important women in your life who influenced you to live the way you do now?
- Are there younger women than you who look up to you right now? How does that make you feel? What do you hope to pass on to those women?

Participant Workbook Discussion Questions

1. Whether we realize it or not, we are always passing things along. Attitudes, habits, and values are constantly being taught, and through that process we leave a legacy to those who have known us. (Day 1, page 172)

- What is a habit, trait, or physical characteristic that was passed down to you that you could have done without? (page 172)
- What is a habit, trait, or physical characteristic that you are thankful was passed down to you? (page 172)
- What is your faith heritage? What views were passed on to you regarding God, Jesus, and the church? (page 173)

2. Timothy plays a significant role in the New Testament, but we probably never would have known of him if it weren't for two very special ladies who were intentional in helping him develop his faith. It is beautiful to read in Paul's second letter to Timothy that from infancy Timothy had been engulfed in the love and teachings of Christ. What a beautiful example to us of how we are to bring up our own children and grandchildren or teach the children God has entrusted to our care or influence. (Day 1, pages 175–76)

- Read 2 Timothy 3:14-17. According to these verses, what did Eunice and Lois teach Timothy? (page 174)
- Who has shaped your faith story or heritage the way that Lois and Eunice shaped Timothy's (regardless of your age)? (page 174)
- When others speak of your legacy, what do you want to be said? (page 175)

3. Just like catching a cold or strep throat, we catch what we're exposed to—what those around us are modeling. Timothy caught what Lois and Eunice demonstrated for him. And our kids, coworkers, friends, and neighbors are going to catch a lot of stuff from us. (Day 2, page 179)

- What traits and habits have you caught from others in your life recently? (page 179)
- Who in your sphere of influence may be catching habits from you today? What habits do you want to model for them? Are there any habits that you would be embarrassed for them to emulate? (page 179)
- Read Deuteronomy 4:9 and Deuteronomy 6:4-9. What do these verses tell us we must do? (page 179)

4. We must make God first priority in our lives. We're not going to be able to pass along godly values if we aren't living them. We are to be intentional in sharing God's love and standards, His commands, with those around us. We have to be show-and-tell Christians— showing our faith in our actions and telling about our Savior through our words. (Day 2, page 180)

- What do you think it means to be a show-and-tell Christian?
- What can we do to make God first priority in our lives?
- What implicit or explicit messages are we sending out by our list of priorities?

5. The purpose of studying God's Word is not just to gain knowledge. Knowledge that is unapplied is a dangerous thing because it can produce pride or a false sense of relationship with God. The goal of studying the Bible is life change. As we read in 2 Timothy, the purpose of incorporating Scripture into our lives is so that it may teach us, correct us, and keep us on a straight path that honors God. It

also brings blessings into our lives as we live out God's Word. (Day 3, page 186)

- Read Deuteronomy 6:4-9; 2 Timothy 2:15; and 2 Timothy 3:16. What is the purpose of incorporating Scripture in our lives? (page 185)
- What can you do to impress God's Word deeper into your own life? (page 185)
- How can you or do you already model the importance of Bible study for those in your sphere of influence? (page 186)

6. [The Bible] doesn't say we will be blessed as we *learn* God's commands but as we *do* them. Lois and Eunice apparently led Timothy to both know and do the will of God. (Day 3, page 186)

- Read John 13:17. According to this verse, when are we blessed by knowledge? (page 186)
- When you think about your influence in others' lives, how do you define your "win"?
- How can we teach others to both know and to do the will of God?

7. By simple definition, prayer is communicating with God. Just as in any other relationship, this will involve both talking and listening. (Day 4, page 189)

- What was prayer like in your home when you were growing up? (page 189)
- How would you describe your prayer life now? (page 189)
- Read Philippians 4:6; John 15:7; and Matthew 6:5-15. What do these verses mean for your life and the lives of those you influence? (pages 189–90)

8. We must be wise about who we allow to shape our hearts and minds—and the hearts and minds of our children. And we must be intentional to build these close relationships so that there is a depth of friendship that allows us to speak kindly but freely in order to correct, advise, and encourage. (Day 4, page 192)

- Read Proverbs 13:20 and Proverbs 27:17. What do these verses mean? (page 192)

- Read Hebrews 10:24-25. What does this passage instruct us to do? (page 192)
- How have close Christian relationships shaped your life? (page 192)

9. As a mom, grandmother, aunt, teacher, or someone else who has influence over others—and we all do—it's important to define what matters most. What does a win look like? In schools, teachers are given benchmarks that each child is to reach by a certain age. It gives the teacher a guideline of how the student is doing and defines the teacher's win as a classroom leader. We, too, need benchmarks so that we know how we're doing and how those around us are faring. (Day 5, page 195)

- Read Deuteronomy 4:9. How does this verse speak to you in your current phase of life? (page 195)
- What additional thoughts do you have about defining your win—as a Christ follower and a person of influence?
- What are some ways to do a benchmark check to see how you are doing with nurturing others in faith?

10. The degree to which these godly characteristics [navigating the Bible, personalizing Scripture, articulating your faith, making wise choices, and displaying the fruit of the Spirit] are evident in our lives is a great benchmark for evaluating our progress. They are the by-products of a heart surrendered to God. (Day 5, page 198)

- Read Galatians 5:22-23. What is the fruit that the Holy Spirit produces in our lives? (page 198)
- Would you say your heart is surrendered to God today? What are the by-products of that surrender that show in your daily life?
- How can you encourage those for whom you have influence to grow in navigating the Bible, personalizing Scripture, articulating faith, making wise choices, and displaying the fruit of the Spirit?

11. We have each been given a heritage, but the legacy we leave for others is ours to choose. Let's choose well. Let's learn from each of the fierce women we have studied, facing the challenges of our lives with the courage of Shiphrah and Puah, the midwives of Egypt; the faith of Naaman's slave girl; the wisdom of Deborah; the humility of the

woman at the well; the compassion of Dorcas; and the intentionality of Lois and Eunice. Let's be fierce! (Day 5, page 200)

- What thoughts or discoveries are sticking with you from studying these fierce women of faith?

Deeper Conversation (15 minutes)

Divide into smaller groups of two or three for deeper conversation. (Encourage the women to break into different groups each week.) Before the session, write on a marker board or chart paper the question or questions you want the groups to discuss:

- Which of the fierce women we've studied are you most drawn to? What about her draws your heart to her story?
- In what ways will you live more fiercely from now on?

Give a two-minute warning before time is up so that the groups may wrap up their discussion.

Closing Prayer (5 minutes)

Close the session by taking personal prayer requests from group members and leading the group in prayer. Encourage members to participate in the closing prayer by praying out loud for one another and the requests given, and invite them to continue praying for one another in the weeks to come.

Video Viewer Guide Answers

Week 1
control
aware / combat
criticism
faithfulness

Week 2
joy / purpose
ourselves / through
excuses

Week 3
kindness / unkind
sin / loves

Week 4
positions
encounter / full
do / respond

Week 5
tapestry
talent / ministry
abilities
gifts / bless / build
experiences / painful

Week 6
pain / ministry
model
mature diciples

Made in the USA
Columbia, SC
26 August 2023

22128782R00037